The Power of Your Words

Cultivating Self-Love Through Positive Self-Talk

ISBN
978-1-7369559-1-8

Circlesquare Projections Publishing Company
Pacoima, Los Angeles, CA, 91331

The Power of Your Words

Cultivating Self-Love Through Positive Self-Talk

Jose Valladares

For Gloria

Contents

About the author:

I'm a multidisciplinary author with a deep curiosity for the world. With a degree in physics, chemistry, and mathematics, I have devoted my life to exploring the mysteries of the universe and seeking to understand the fundamental laws that govern our existence.

However, my interests extend far beyond the scientific realm. I am also an accomplished musician, having released nine albums that showcase my passion for playing the piano. When not writing or playing music, I devote time to prayer, seeking spiritual guidance and inspiration from our Lord Jesus.

As a prolific author, I have published over 46 books that cover a diverse range of topics, from coloring books, poetry, philosophy, music, science and spirituality to personal growth and transformation. My aim as a writer is to spread positivity and love, and to motivate others to live their best lives.

Currently residing in the dynamic city of Los Angeles, California, I am eager to connect with readers like you and embark on a journey of discovery and growth together.

Preface:

I am excited to share with you this book on self-love, a topic that is close to my heart. Throughout my life, I have struggled with negative self-talk and self-doubt, but through my personal journey, I have discovered the transformative power of self-love.

The purpose of this book is to help you understand the importance of self-love, identify negative self-talk patterns, develop positive self-talk techniques, and embrace your imperfections. Additionally, you will learn how to let go of self-doubt, celebrate your strengths, and build a supportive self-talk environment.

My hope is that this book will serve as a guide and a source of inspiration for those seeking to cultivate a more positive and compassionate relationship with themselves. By practicing self-love, we can improve our overall well-being, boost our self-confidence, and live a more fulfilling life.

In this book, you will find practical tools, strategies, and examples of daily self-love practices and positive affirmations that you can incorporate into your life. I encourage you to read and apply these practices early in the morning, afternoon, and evening to fully integrate self-love into your daily routine.

Thank you for choosing to embark on this journey towards self-love with me.

Introduction

Self-love is a concept that is often misunderstood or overlooked in our society. Many of us may associate self-love with narcissism or selfishness, but in reality, it is a vital component of our overall wellbeing. Self-love is the foundation for a healthy and fulfilling life, and it encompasses everything from positive self-talk to embracing our imperfections and celebrating our strengths. This book is a guide to understanding and cultivating self-love, with a focus on practical techniques and strategies that anyone can implement in their daily life.

In addition to discussing the various components of self-love, I will also be including positive affirmations throughout the book. The power of positive self-talk is something I truly believe in. By speaking kindly to myself and practicing affirmations, I am able to build my self-confidence and improve my overall well-being. These affirmations are recommended to be read early in the morning, afternoon, and evening to maximize their impact.

1
Understanding the Importance of Self-Love

Why Self-Love is Important

S elf-love is a crucial aspect of our overall well-being. It is the foundation for healthy relationships, emotional resilience, and mental health. Without self-love, we may struggle to find meaning and purpose in our lives and may find it challenging to form deep connections with others.

In this chapter, we will explore the importance of self-love and how it can positively impact our lives. We will also discuss the consequences of neglecting self-love and how it can lead to negative thought patterns and self-destructive behaviors.

1.1 Defining Self-Love

Self-love is the practice of accepting and nurturing oneself, including our strengths and flaws, with kindness, compassion, and respect. It involves recognizing our inherent worth and treating ourselves with the same care and attention we would offer to someone we love.

Self-love is different from self-esteem, which refers to our overall evaluation of ourselves, our sense of personal worth, and how we perceive our abilities and achievements. Self-esteem can fluctuate based on external factors such as success, approval, or social comparison, whereas self-love is rooted in the unconditional acceptance of oneself, regardless of external circumstances.

Self-love and self-esteem are like the roots and trunk of a tree. The roots, like self-love, provide the necessary nutrients and support for the tree to grow and thrive. Self-love provides the foundation for our emotional well-being and helps us to accept and care for ourselves unconditionally.

The trunk, like self-esteem, represents the strength and stability of the tree. Self-esteem is the belief and confidence we have in ourselves, and it allows us to stand tall and weather the storms of life. Just as a strong trunk is essential for a healthy tree, strong self-esteem is essential for a healthy self-image and overall mental health.

Together, self-love and self-esteem form a symbiotic relationship that is necessary for personal growth and fulfillment. Without self-love, our self-esteem may suffer, and without self-esteem, our self-love may be superficial and lacking in substance. Like a tree, we need both to thrive and reach our full potential.

The relationship between self-love and self-care is also important. Self-care is the practice of taking intentional actions to care for oneself physically, mentally, and emotionally. It includes activities such as getting enough sleep, eating healthy, engaging in physical activity, and seeking professional help when needed. Self-love is the foundation for self-care, as it requires recognizing and honoring our needs and taking action to meet them in a way that is compassionate and nurturing.

Self-love and self-care are like two sides of the same coin. Just as a coin has two faces, self-love and self-care work together to create a healthy and balanced life.

Self-love is like the foundation of a building, it provides the support and stability needed for the structure to stand tall. Similarly, self-love is the foundation of a healthy life. It is about recognizing your own worth and treating yourself with kindness and compassion.

Self-care is like the bricks and mortar that make up the building. Without these elements, the foundation alone cannot create a functional structure. Similarly, self-care is the actions that we take to nurture and care for ourselves. It includes practices such as eating well, getting enough sleep, and exercising regularly.

Just as a building needs both a strong foundation and solid structure, we need both self-love and self-care to create a healthy and fulfilling life. Self-love provides the foundation, while self-care provides the structure, and together they form the basis for a strong and resilient life.

Self-love is the practice of treating ourselves with kindness, compassion, and respect, recognizing our inherent worth, and honoring our needs. It is distinct from self-esteem, which refers to our evaluation of ourselves, and is the foundation for self-care.

1.2 The Benefits of Self-Love

Self-love has numerous benefits for our mental, physical, and emotional well-being.

Here are some of the ways that self-love can have a positive impact on our lives:

The Positive Impact of Self-Love on Mental Health

Self-love is an essential component of our overall well-being, and it has a significant impact on our mental health. When we cultivate self-love, we increase our self-esteem and confidence, reduce negative self-talk and self-criticism, promote a positive outlook on life, decrease anxiety and depression symptoms, and improve our emotional regulation and coping skills.

One of the most significant benefits of self-love is that it increases our self-esteem and confidence. When we practice self-love, we recognize our inherent worth and value, and we learn to appreciate ourselves for who we are, including our strengths and flaws. This recognition helps us to feel more confident in ourselves and our abilities, which in turn leads to a more positive outlook on life. One way to improve self-esteem and confidence is to set achievable goals and work towards them. When you set goals and take steps to achieve them, it can give you a sense of accomplishment and increase your self-confidence. Start with small, achievable goals, and then gradually increase the difficulty level as you gain confidence. Celebrate your successes, no matter how small they may be, and use them as motivation to continue growing and improving. Remember that self-esteem and confidence are not built overnight, but rather through consistent effort and practice.

Another benefit of self-love is that it reduces negative self-talk and self-criticism. Negative self-talk and self-criticism can be damaging to our mental health, leading to feelings of anxiety, depression, and low self-esteem. When we practice self-love, we learn to be kinder to ourselves and to replace negative self-talk with positive affirmations, leading to a more positive and optimistic outlook on life.

Negative self-talk and self-criticism are like weeds in a garden. Just as weeds can choke out the beauty and growth of a garden, negative self-talk and self-criticism can smother our self-esteem and confidence. Just as it's important to pull weeds from a garden to allow plants to flourish, it's important to recognize negative self-talk and self-criticism and work to eliminate them to allow our self-esteem and confidence to thrive.

One way to reduce self-criticism is to practice self-compassion. Instead of being overly critical of yourself, try to treat yourself with the same kindness and understanding that you would offer to a friend. Recognize that everyone makes mistakes and has flaws, and try to respond to your own shortcomings with patience and forgiveness. Focus on your positive qualities and accomplishments rather than dwelling on your perceived failures or inadequacies. Remember that self-criticism can be a vicious cycle, and by treating yourself with compassion and understanding, you can break free from this cycle and build greater self-esteem and confidence.

Furthermore, self-love can also decrease anxiety and depression symptoms. Anxiety and depression are common mental health issues that can have a significant impact on our daily lives. Practicing self-love can help reduce the symptoms of these conditions by promoting a sense of calm and well-being, improving our emotional regulation skills, and encouraging us to engage in activities that bring us joy and fulfillment.

Self-love can also improve our emotional regulation and coping skills. When we practice self-love, we learn to recognize and accept our emotions without judgment or criticism. This recognition helps us to regulate our emotions more effectively, leading to greater emotional stability and resilience. Moreover, self-love encourages us to develop healthy coping skills, such as seeking social support, engaging in physical activity, or practicing mindfulness, which can help us navigate life's challenges with more ease and grace.

Therefore, self-love is a critical component of our mental health and well-being. It helps to increase our self-esteem and confidence, reduce negative self-talk and self-criticism, promote a positive outlook on life, decrease anxiety and depression symptoms, and improve our emotional regulation and coping skills. By practicing self-love, we can cultivate a greater sense of calm, well-being, and resilience, leading to a more fulfilling and happy life.

The Impact of Self-Love on Physical Health and Well-Being

Self-love is not only essential for our mental health but also has a significant impact on our physical health and well-being. When we practice self-love, we can lower our blood pressure and reduce the risk of heart disease, boost our immune system functioning, improve our sleep quality and duration, reduce stress levels and promote relaxation, and enhance our overall physical health and well-being.

One of the most significant benefits of self-love is its ability to lower blood pressure and reduce the risk of heart disease. High blood pressure is a common health problem that can lead to more severe conditions such as heart disease, stroke, or kidney failure. Practicing self-love, such as engaging in physical activity, eating a healthy diet, and managing stress levels, can help reduce blood pressure and lower the risk of heart disease.

Another benefit of self-love is its ability to boost our immune system functioning. Our immune system is responsible for fighting off diseases and infections, and it plays a crucial role in maintaining our overall health and well-being. When we practice self-love, such as getting enough sleep, eating a nutritious diet, and engaging in physical activity, we can boost our immune system functioning and reduce our risk of illnesses and infections.

Moreover, self-love can also improve our sleep quality and duration. Sleep is essential for our physical health and well-being, and it plays a crucial role in our mental health as well. When we practice self-love, such as maintaining a consistent sleep schedule, reducing screen time before bed, and engaging in relaxation techniques, we can improve our sleep quality and duration, leading to greater energy, focus, and overall well-being.

Self-love can also reduce stress levels and promote relaxation. Stress is a common health problem that can lead to numerous negative health consequences, including heart disease, anxiety, and depression. When we practice self-love, such as engaging in relaxation techniques like meditation, deep breathing, or yoga, we can reduce stress levels and promote relaxation, leading to greater emotional well-being and overall physical health.

For example, if someone practices self-love by taking time to engage in physical activity they enjoy, such as yoga or hiking, they can improve their physical health by reducing their risk of heart disease, boosting their immune system, and reducing stress levels. This, in turn, can lead to an overall improvement in their well-being and a happier, more fulfilling life.

The Role of Self-Love in Building Resilience and Coping with Stress

Self-love is an essential component of building resilience and coping with stress. When we practice self-love, we increase our ability to bounce back from challenges, promote healthy coping mechanisms, encourage self-compassion and forgiveness, and enhance our problem-solving skills and creative thinking. These skills are critical to navigating life's challenges with more ease and grace.

One of the most significant benefits of self-love is its ability to increase resilience and the ability to bounce back from challenges. Life is full of ups and downs, and it can be challenging to maintain a positive outlook when faced with adversity. When we practice self-love, we develop a sense of self-worth and confidence that can help us to overcome challenges and bounce back from setbacks with greater ease.

Self-love promotes healthy coping mechanisms, such as seeking social support or engaging in physical activity. Coping mechanisms are essential to managing stress and building resilience. When we practice self-love, we learn to recognize and honor our needs, including the need for support and self-care. This recognition helps us to develop healthy coping mechanisms that can help us manage stress and maintain our emotional well-being.

Another benefit of self-love is its ability to encourage self-compassion and forgiveness. Self-compassion and forgiveness are critical to reducing the impact of stress on our lives. When we practice self-love, we learn to be kinder to ourselves and to forgive ourselves for our mistakes and shortcomings. This self-compassion and forgiveness can help us to reduce stress and increase our emotional resilience.

Just as forgiveness involves letting go of the anger and resentment we hold towards others for their mistakes, self-compassion involves letting go of the negative self-talk and self-blame that we hold towards ourselves for our own mistakes.

For example, imagine you made a mistake at work that resulted in some negative consequences. If you practice self-compassion, you would acknowledge the mistake, take responsibility for it, and offer yourself kindness and understanding. You would recognize that everyone makes mistakes and that it doesn't define your worth as a person. In the same way, if you were forgiving someone for a mistake they made, you would acknowledge their mistake,

take responsibility for your own emotions, and offer them kindness and understanding. You would recognize that they are human and capable of making mistakes, and that holding onto anger and resentment is only hurting yourself.

In both cases, self-compassion and forgiveness involve acknowledging our own imperfections and treating ourselves (and others) with kindness, understanding, and empathy.

Finally, self-love enhances problem-solving skills and creative thinking, which can help us navigate difficult situations with more ease. When we practice self-love, we learn to trust ourselves and our abilities, which can help us to think creatively and find new solutions to challenges. This creative thinking can help us to navigate difficult situations with more ease, leading to greater resilience and emotional well-being.

One way to improve creative thinking is to engage in activities that challenge your mind and encourage you to think outside of the box. For example, you could try brainstorming exercises where you come up with as many ideas as possible, even if they seem unconventional or silly at first. You could also try doing puzzles, playing strategy games, or taking up a new hobby that requires you to use your imagination and problem-solving skills. Another helpful practice is to expose yourself to new experiences and perspectives, such as traveling to new places or reading books on topics you are unfamiliar with. By continually challenging your mind and expanding your horizons, you can develop a more creative and innovative mindset.

Self-love is crucial in developing resilience and managing stress. By improving our capability to recover from obstacles, promoting healthy coping strategies, practicing self-compassion and forgiveness, and improving problem-solving abilities and creativity, self-love can aid us in facing life's obstacles more smoothly and elegantly. By nurturing self-love, we can build stronger resilience, maintain our emotional well-being, and live happier and more satisfying lives.

Practicing self-love can offer various advantages for our mental, physical, and emotional wellness. It can lead to positive self-talk, enhance our immune system, and improve our overall health and well-being. Additionally, self-love can play an essential part in developing resilience and coping with stress, enabling us to handle life's obstacles more smoothly and gracefully.

1.3 The Consequences of Neglecting Self-Love

Neglecting self-love can have severe consequences on our mental and emotional well-being. The dangers of negative self-talk and self-criticism, the link between low self-love and depression and anxiety, and how neglecting self-love can lead to unhealthy behaviors and relationships are some of the consequences of neglecting self-love.

One of the most significant consequences of neglecting self-love is negative self-talk and self-criticism. Negative self-talk and self-criticism can be damaging to our mental and emotional health, leading to feelings of low self-esteem, anxiety, and depression. When we neglect self-love, we tend to focus on our flaws and shortcomings, leading to negative self-talk and self-criticism, which can be detrimental to our mental and emotional health.

Negative self-talk can be compared to a storm cloud that hovers over our heads, constantly raining down criticism and judgment. Similarly, self-criticism can be seen as a storm that hits our emotional landscape, leaving us feeling battered and defeated. Both negative self-talk and self-criticism can be damaging to our self-esteem and confidence, leading to feelings of inadequacy and self-doubt. However, just as we can take steps to weather a storm, we can also learn to manage and reduce negative self-talk and self-criticism through techniques such as mindfulness, self-compassion, and positive affirmations.

The link between low self-love and depression and anxiety is well-established. When we neglect self-love, we tend to have a negative view of ourselves, which can lead to feelings of worthlessness, hopelessness, and helplessness, all of which are symptoms of depression and anxiety. Research has shown that individuals who have low self-esteem or low self-love are more likely to experience anxiety and depression than those who have a positive view of themselves.

Depression, on the other hand, is a mental health condition characterized by persistent feelings of sadness, hopelessness, and loss of interest in daily activities. It can affect a person's mood, thoughts, behavior, and physical health. Depression can make it difficult to experience joy, pleasure, and positive emotions.

Anxiety is a feeling of fear or unease about a future event or situation. It can be a normal and adaptive response to stress, but when it becomes excessive or uncontrollable, it can interfere with daily life. Anxiety can manifest as physical symptoms such as increased heart rate, sweating, and trembling.

While self-love can contribute to better mental and emotional well-being, depression and anxiety are mental health conditions that require professional treatment. It's important to recognize the differences between these concepts and seek appropriate help when needed.

Neglecting self-love can also lead to unhealthy behaviors and relationships. When we do not have a positive relationship with ourselves, we may engage in self-destructive behaviors, such as substance abuse or overeating, to cope with negative emotions. We may also form unhealthy relationships, seeking validation from others rather than learning to validate ourselves. This can lead to a cycle of low self-esteem and negative self-talk, reinforcing our negative beliefs about ourselves.

In conclusion, neglecting self-love can have significant consequences on our mental and emotional well-being. Negative self-talk and self-criticism, depression and anxiety, and unhealthy behaviors and relationships are some of the consequences of neglecting self-love. It is essential to cultivate self-love by learning to accept and appreciate ourselves, practicing self-care and mindfulness, and engaging in activities that bring us joy and fulfillment. By cultivating self-love, we can improve our mental and emotional well-being, leading to a happier and more fulfilling life.

1.4 Cultivating Self-love

Cultivating self-love is an essential part of maintaining our mental and emotional well-being. Developing a positive relationship with ourselves, practicing mindfulness, and practicing self-compassion and forgiveness are all strategies for cultivating self-love.

One of the most important strategies for developing a positive relationship with yourself is to practice self-care. Self-care involves taking care of our physical, emotional, and mental health. Some examples of self-care include engaging in physical activity, eating a nutritious diet, getting enough sleep, practicing relaxation techniques, and engaging in activities that bring us joy and fulfillment.

Another strategy for developing a positive relationship with yourself is to engage in self-reflection. Self-reflection involves examining our thoughts, feelings, and behaviors without judgment. By practicing self-reflection, we can become more aware of our emotions and our thought patterns, allowing us to identify negative self-talk and self-criticism and replace it with positive affirmations.

The role of mindfulness in cultivating self-love is also crucial. Mindfulness involves paying attention to the present moment without judgment. When we practice mindfulness, we learn to be more present and aware of our thoughts and emotions, helping us to recognize negative self-talk and self-criticism and replace it with positive affirmations. Mindfulness can also help us to develop greater self-awareness, leading to a greater understanding of ourselves and our needs.

An example of mindfulness could be taking a few minutes to sit quietly and focus on your breath, noticing each inhale and exhale without judging or analyzing them. During this time, you may become aware of distracting thoughts or feelings, but instead of dwelling on them, you acknowledge them and then gently bring your attention back to your breath. By practicing mindfulness regularly, you can develop greater awareness of your thoughts and emotions, and learn to respond to them in a more compassionate and non-judgmental way, which can lead to increased self-love and emotional well-being.

Practicing self-compassion and forgiveness is another essential strategy for cultivating self-love. Self-compassion involves learning to be kinder to ourselves and to treat ourselves with the same kindness and compassion we would offer to others. Forgiveness involves learning to forgive ourselves for our mistakes and short-comings. By practicing self-compassion and forgiveness, we can reduce negative self-talk and self-criticism and increase our sense of self-worth and self-love.

Developing a positive relationship with ourselves is essential for maintaining our mental and emotional well-being. Engaging in self-reflection and self-care are two strategies that can help us appreciate and accept ourselves. Another critical strategy is mindfulness, which can enable us to recognize negative self-talk and self-criticism and replace them with positive affirmations. Practicing self-compassion and forgiveness is also crucial for cultivating self-love, as it can reduce negative self-talk and enhance our sense of self-worth and self-love. By nurturing self-love, we can enhance our mental and emotional well-being, leading to a more fulfilling and happier life.

Why Self-Love is Essential

Self-love is essential for maintaining our mental and emotional well-being. It is the foundation upon which we build our sense of self-worth and self-confidence. In this essay, we will recap the importance of self-love, I encourage readers to prioritize self-love in their daily lives, and how developing self-love can lead to a more fulfilling and happy life.

Self-love is essential for maintaining our mental and emotional well-being. When we love ourselves, we develop a positive relationship with ourselves, allowing us to appreciate and accept ourselves as we are. This positive relationship can help us to navigate life's challenges with greater ease and grace, leading to greater resilience and emotional well-being.

Moreover, self-love is crucial for building our self-confidence and self-esteem. When we love ourselves, we learn to trust ourselves and our abilities, leading to greater confidence and self-assurance. This self-confidence can help us to pursue our goals and dreams with greater determination and perseverance, leading to greater fulfillment and success.

I encouraging readers to prioritize self-love in their daily lives is crucial for maintaining their mental and emotional well-being. This can involve engaging in self-care activities, practicing mindfulness, engaging in positive self-talk, and practicing self-compassion and forgiveness. By prioritizing self-love, readers can develop a positive relationship with themselves, increase their self-confidence, and reduce negative self-talk and self-criticism.

Developing self-love can also lead to a more fulfilling and happy life. By learning to love ourselves, we can build healthier relationships with others, as we are better able to love and accept them as they are. We can also pursue our passions and interests with greater determination and enjoyment, leading to greater fulfillment and happiness.

It is essential for maintaining our mental and emotional well-being, building our self-confidence and self-esteem, and leading to a more fulfilling and happy life. By prioritizing self-love in our daily lives, we can develop a positive relationship with ourselves, reduce negative self-talk and self-criticism, and increase our sense of self-worth and self-love. By loving and accepting ourselves, we can lead happier, healthier, and more fulfilling lives.

The Power of Positive Self Talk

The power of positive self-talk is something I truly believe in. By speaking kindly to myself and practicing affirmations, I am able to build my self-confidence and improve my overall well-being. When I engage in negative self-talk, it only brings me down and causes unnecessary stress and anxiety. But by intentionally replacing negative thoughts with positive ones, I am able to shift my mindset and cultivate a more positive and self-loving attitude. Positive self-talk helps me to stay motivated, focus on my strengths, and see challenges as opportunities for growth. It is a powerful tool that I use every day to improve my mental and emotional health.

In the morning as soon as you wake up read these sentences to improve your self-love, and mental health.

I am a unique and valuable creation, worthy of love and respect. I am proud of myself for being who I am and for all that I have accomplished. My strengths and weaknesses make me who I am, and I love and accept myself just as I am. I am a beautiful and precious being, with a unique purpose and mission in this world. When I struggle or experience pain, I know that I have the power to seek support and guidance to help me through it. My mistakes and failures do not define me, and they do not diminish my worth or value in any way. I am deserving of love, happiness, and fulfillment, and I am committed to working towards these goals. I am a child of the universe, and I have a divine spark within me that shines brightly. I believe in myself, and I know that I am capable of achieving great things in this life. I am loved, cherished, and valued beyond measure, and nothing can ever change that.

2

Identifying Negative Self-Talk

In order to cultivate self-love and build a positive relationship with ourselves, it is essential to be aware of and recognize negative self-talk. Negative self-talk is the inner dialogue that we have with ourselves, which can be critical, judgmental, and self-deprecating. Just as plants require water, sun, and nutrients to thrive, our inner voice also needs nourishment and care to support our mental and emotional well-being.

Negative self-talk can be compared to depriving a plant of water, while positive self-talk is like providing it with the necessary nutrients and sunlight. By nurturing our inner voice with positivity and kindness, we can help it grow and flourish, just as we care for our plants. Just as plants can't survive without water, sun, and nutrients, we can't thrive without a healthy and supportive inner voice.

In this chapter, we will explore how to identify negative self-talk and its impact on our mental and emotional well-being.

2.1 Defining Negative Self-Talk

The way we talk to ourselves can have a significant impact on our mental and emotional well-being. Negative self-talk is a common issue that many of us struggle with, but it can be challenging to recognize and address. In this essay, we will explore what negative self-talk is, how to identify it, and the impact it can have on our mental and emotional health.

Negative self-talk is the internal voice that tells us we are not good enough, smart enough, or talented enough. It can be subtle and automatic, often going unnoticed or dismissed as just a passing thought. However, over time, negative self-talk can become a habit that erodes our self-esteem and confidence. Negative self-talk can take many forms, such as self-criticism, self-doubt, and self-blame.

One way to identify negative self-talk is to pay attention to our inner dialogue. What do we say to ourselves when we make a mistake or encounter a challenge? Do we immediately jump to self-criticism or self-blame? Do we engage in black-and-white thinking, where everything is either good or bad, right or wrong, with no room for shades of gray? These are all signs of negative self-talk.

Another way to identify negative self-talk is to notice our physical and emotional reactions to our thoughts. When we engage in negative self-talk, we may feel anxious, stressed, or depressed. We may also experience physical symptoms, such as headaches, stomachaches, or muscle tension. Paying attention to our reactions can help us identify negative self-talk and its impact on our well-being.

The impact of negative self-talk on our mental and emotional well-being cannot be overstated. Negative self-talk can lead to feelings of anxiety, depression, and low self-esteem. It can also affect our relationships with others, as we may become more critical and judgmental towards them. Negative self-talk can also lead to self-sabotaging behaviors and affect our ability to achieve our goals.

To overcome negative self-talk, we must first become aware of it. This requires us to pay attention to our thoughts, reactions, and behaviors. We must then challenge our negative self-talk by asking ourselves if our thoughts are based on facts or assumptions. We can also reframe our negative thoughts into positive affirmations, such as "I am capable and competent" or "I am worthy of love and respect." Practicing self-compassion is also essential, as it involves treating ourselves with kindness and understanding, recognizing that we are human and imperfect.

Recognizing and addressing negative self-talk is a crucial component of developing a positive self-image and practicing self-love. Negative self-talk can have detrimental effects on our mental and emotional health, making it vital to identify and challenge these thoughts. By consciously acknowledging and reframing our negative self-talk, as well as showing ourselves compassion, we can overcome these harmful thought patterns and strengthen our self-esteem and confidence.

2.2 Types of Negative Self-Talk

Negative self-talk can take many different forms and can be challenging to recognize and overcome. We will explore some of the different types of negative self-talk and their impact on our mental and emotional well-being.

One common type of negative self-talk is catastrophizing. This involves imagining the worst-case scenario and assuming that it will inevitably happen. For example, if we have an upcoming job interview, we may catastrophize by imagining that we will forget everything we wanted to say or that we will embarrass ourselves in some way. This type of negative self-talk can lead to anxiety and stress, as we become fixated on the worst-case scenario and overlook other possible outcomes.

Another type of negative self-talk is personalizing. This involves taking responsibility for things that are outside of our control and blaming ourselves for things that are not our fault. For example, if a friend cancels plans, we may personalize the situation by assuming that they don't want to spend time with us because we are not interesting enough. This type of negative self-talk can lead to feelings of guilt and shame, as we blame ourselves for things that are not within our control.

One way I can prevent personalizing is by practicing self-reflection and examining my thoughts and beliefs. I can ask myself if there is evidence to support my belief that I am responsible for something negative that has happened, or if I am taking something personally when it is not actually about me. I can also challenge my assumptions and consider alternative explanations for the situation. Additionally, seeking the perspective of others can provide valuable insight and help me to avoid personalizing situations.

Overgeneralizing is another type of negative self-talk that involves making sweeping statements about ourselves based on a single negative experience. For example, if we make a mistake at work, we may overgeneralize by assuming that we are not good at our job and never will be. This type of negative self-talk can lead to low self-esteem and a lack of confidence, as we assume that one negative experience defines our entire worth or ability.

One way I can prevent overgeneralizing is to focus on the specific details and circumstances of a situation, rather than making broad generalizations based on one experience. For example, instead of saying "I always mess things up," I can focus on specific instances where I may have made mistakes and identify what I can do differently in the future. This can help to challenge my negative self-talk and prevent overgeneralizing.

Finally, labeling is a type of negative self-talk that involves using negative labels to describe ourselves or others. For example, we may label ourselves as "lazy," "stupid," or "failure." This type of negative self-talk can lead to self-fulfilling prophecies, where we start to believe that the labels we apply to ourselves are true and act accordingly.

To prevent labeling, one approach is to practice mindfulness and observe our thoughts without judgment. We can try to avoid using extreme labels or terms that are overly critical of ourselves or others. Instead, we can try to describe specific behaviors or actions without making generalizations about a person's character. It can also be helpful to challenge our assumptions and consider alternative explanations for behavior before labeling someone or ourselves. Additionally, seeking the perspective of others can provide valuable insight and help us avoid labeling.

It is crucial to identify the various forms of negative self-talk to challenge them effectively. Different types of negative self-talk, such as catastrophizing, personalizing, overgeneralizing, and labeling, can have a significant impact on our mental and emotional well-being, so we need to recognize and address them. By reframing our negative thoughts, practicing self-compassion, and seeking support from others, we can overcome negative self-talk and develop a positive relationship with ourselves, leading to increased self-esteem and confidence.

2.3 The Impact of Negative Self-Talk

The way we talk to ourselves can have a significant impact on our mental and emotional well-being. Negative self-talk, which is the inner voice that tells us we are not good enough, smart enough, or talented enough, can have a particularly detrimental effect. In this essay, we will explore the impact of negative self-talk on our mental and emotional health.

Negative self-talk can contribute to feelings of anxiety, depression, and low self-esteem. When we engage in negative self-talk, we reinforce the belief that we are not good enough, which can lead to feelings of inadequacy and self-doubt. This can contribute to anxiety, as we worry about not measuring up to our own or others' expectations. It can also contribute to depression, as we feel helpless and hopeless in the face of our negative thoughts.

Negative self-talk can also lead to self-sabotaging behaviors. When we believe that we are not good enough, we may engage in behaviors that reinforce this belief, such as procrastination or avoidance. This can lead to a lack of progress towards our goals and a sense of disappointment in ourselves.

It can also affect our ability to achieve our goals. When we engage in negative self-talk, we may become discouraged and give up on pursuing our goals. We may also set lower goals for ourselves, believing that we are not capable of achieving more.

Just like we take care of our plants by providing them with water, sun, and nutrients to help them grow and flourish, we can nurture our inner voice with positivity and kindness to help it become healthy and supportive. For example, when we make a mistake, instead of engaging in negative self-talk, we can practice self-compassion and remind ourselves that everyone makes mistakes and that it is an opportunity for growth and learning. By taking care of our inner voice, we can improve our mental and emotional well-being and lead happier, more fulfilling lives.

The effects of negative self-talk on our mental and emotional well-being are significant. It can contribute to feelings of anxiety, depression, and low self-esteem, which can hinder our ability to reach our goals. Therefore, it is crucial to identify and challenge negative self-talk by becoming mindful of our thoughts, changing negative thoughts into positive affirmations, and practicing self-compassion. By doing so, we can develop self-love and create a healthier relationship with ourselves.

2.4 Strategies for Overcoming Negative Self-Talk

Negative self-talk can be a significant obstacle to our overall well-being and happiness. Fortunately, there are several strategies that we can use to overcome negative self-talk and cultivate a more positive relationship with ourselves. In this essay, we will explore some of the most effective strategies for overcoming negative self-talk.

The first strategy for overcoming negative self-talk is self-awareness. Becoming aware of our negative self-talk is the first step in overcoming it. We must learn to identify the negative messages that we send ourselves and recognize when we engage in self-criticism, self-doubt, or self-blame.

Self-awareness is the first step in overcoming negative self-talk. It involves recognizing when negative self-talk is occurring and being mindful of the thoughts and feelings associated with it. For example, if you notice yourself thinking, "I can't do anything right," you can become aware of this thought and the impact it may be having on your mood and behavior. Once you are aware of the negative self-talk, you can challenge it and replace it with more positive and affirming self-talk, such as "I am capable and can learn from my mistakes."

The second strategy for overcoming negative self-talk is mindfulness. Practicing mindfulness can help us become more aware of our thoughts and emotions, allowing us to recognize negative self-talk and replace it with positive affirmations. Mindfulness involves paying attention to the present moment, non-judgmentally, and with acceptance. This can help us to become more aware of our negative self-talk and create space for more positive and supportive thoughts. For example, during a negative self-talk episode, one can take a deep breath and observe their thoughts without reacting to them or allowing them to control their emotions. By staying present and mindful, individuals can identify their negative self-talk patterns and work towards reframing them into positive self-affirmations.

The third strategy for overcoming negative self-talk is reframing. Reframing involves taking negative thoughts and turning them into positive affirmations. For example, instead of saying "I'm not good enough," we can reframe that thought into "I am capable and competent." Reframing our negative thoughts can help us to cultivate self-love and increase our self-esteem. For example, if the thought "I'm not good enough" arises, a person can reframe it as "I am capable of growth and improvement" or "I have strengths and qualities that make me valuable." By reframing negative thoughts, a person can challenge and replace them with more positive and empowering ones.

The fourth strategy for overcoming negative self-talk is self-compassion. Practicing self-compassion involves treating ourselves with kindness and understanding, recognizing that we are human and imperfect. We can practice self-compassion by speaking to ourselves in a gentle and supportive tone, acknowledging our mistakes and limitations without judgment, and recognizing that everyone makes mistakes. An example of practicing self-compassion is to talk to ourselves like we would to a close friend who is going through a tough time. Instead of berating ourselves for making a mistake, we can acknowledge our feelings, reassure ourselves that we are doing the best we can, and offer ourselves words of encouragement and support. By treating ourselves with compassion, we can reduce the impact of negative self-talk on our mental and emotional well-being, and cultivate a more positive relationship with ourselves.

In conclusion, to overcome negative self-talk, it's important to use a multi-faceted approach that involves self-awareness, mindfulness, and self-compassion. We can start by becoming more aware of our negative self-talk and using mindfulness to recognize and reframe these thoughts. By showing ourselves compassion and reframing our negative self-talk into positive affirmations, we can build a more positive relationship with ourselves. With these powerful strategies in place, we can boost our self-esteem, promote our mental and emotional well-being, and lead a happier and more fulfilling life.

Self-talk to Overcome Negative Talk

Every morning as soon as you wake up read these sentences to overcome negative talk, and improve self love.

As I navigate through life, I often struggle with negative self-talk that can bring me down and diminish my self-worth. However, if I remind myself of the loving words that God would say to me as His creation, I can combat negative self-talk and cultivate self-love and acceptance.

Firstly, I need to remind myself that I am loved beyond measure, just as I am. My worth is not determined by my achievements or my mistakes, but by the inherent value that I possess as a unique and precious creation. This affirmation can help me recognize my worth and increase my self-esteem. I can trust that I am enough just as I am and that I do not need validation from others.

Secondly, I need to remember that I am not alone in my struggles. God is always with me, guiding and supporting me through every challenge and every triumph. He sees my pain, and He is here to help me heal. This reminder can bring me comfort and peace, knowing that I have a source of strength and support to turn to in times of need.

Thirdly, I need to believe in myself and trust in the strength and resilience that God has placed within me. I am capable of great things, and I should not let my fears or doubts hold me back. This affirmation can help me overcome self-doubt and believe in my abilities and potential. I can draw strength from the knowledge that I have the power to achieve my goals and overcome any obstacles that come my way.

Fourthly, I need to accept that I am forgiven. My past mistakes do not define me, and I do not need to carry the weight of guilt or shame. God offers me His grace and mercy, and I can extend that same compassion and forgiveness to myself. This reminder can help me let go of my past and embrace self-compassion and forgiveness.

Fifthly, I need to remind myself that I am enough. I do not need to strive for perfection or compare myself to others. I am uniquely gifted and valued, and every part of who I am is worth celebrating. This affirmation can help me accept myself and cultivate self-love. I can appreciate my strengths and embrace my flaws, knowing that they make me who I am.

Sixthly, I need to recognize that I am worthy of love and respect. I should not let anyone else's words or actions make me doubt my worth or my right to be treated with kindness and compassion. This reminder can help me set healthy boundaries and cultivate self-respect. I can stand up for myself and demand to be treated with the love and respect that I deserve.

Finally, I need to remind myself that I am not defined by my struggles or my failures. I am defined by my courage, resilience, and capacity for love and compassion. I can keep moving forward, knowing that God is with me every step of the way. I can trust in His guidance and draw strength from His love, knowing that I have the power to overcome any challenge that comes my way.

In conclusion, by reminding myself of the loving words that God would say to me, I can combat negative self-talk and cultivate self-love and acceptance. By embracing these affirmations, I can increase my self-esteem, improve my mental and emotional well-being, and live a happier and more fulfilling life.

3
The Art of Positive Self-Talk

3.1 Defining Positive Self-talk and its Benefits

Positive self-talk is the practice of intentionally using positive and affirming language to encourage and uplift oneself. This practice can have numerous benefits for mental and emotional well-being, such as reducing stress and anxiety, improving self-esteem, and promoting resilience in the face of challenges.

Positive self-talk is a powerful practice that can have a significant impact on one's mental and emotional well-being. It involves intentionally using positive and affirming language to encourage and uplift oneself, rather than engaging in negative self-talk. Positive self-talk has been shown to have numerous benefits, including reducing stress and anxiety, improving self-esteem, and promoting resilience in the face of challenges.

When we engage in positive self-talk, we shift our mindset towards positivity and optimism. Instead of focusing on our weaknesses or shortcomings, we focus on our strengths and capabilities. This can help improve our self-esteem and self-worth, as we begin to see ourselves in a more positive light. Positive self-talk can also reduce stress and anxiety, as we learn to approach challenges with a more optimistic and solution-focused mindset. For example, instead of saying "I can't do this," we can say "I may find this challenging, but I can learn and grow from the experience." This shift in perspective can have a profound impact on our overall mental and emotional well-being.

Additionally, positive self-talk can promote resilience in the face of challenges. When we practice positive self-talk regularly, we develop a more optimistic outlook on life and are better able to bounce back from setbacks and failures. This can help us approach challenges with a sense of determination and belief in ourselves, rather than giving in to feelings of hopelessness or defeat.

In summary, intentional use of positive self-talk can be highly beneficial for our mental and emotional well-being. When we choose to use positive and affirming language to uplift ourselves, we can lower stress and anxiety levels, boost our self-esteem, and increase our resilience when dealing with difficult situations. By cultivating a more positive mindset through positive self-talk, we can lead a happier and more fulfilling life.

3.2 Techniques for Developing Positive Self-talk

Developing positive self-talk can be a life-changing practice for improving mental and emotional well-being. There are several techniques that one can use to develop positive self-talk, including reframing negative thoughts, practicing gratitude, using positive affirmations, and visualizing success.

Reframing negative thoughts is a powerful technique for developing positive self-talk. When negative thoughts arise, try to reframe them into positive self-talk. For example, instead of thinking "I'm not good enough," try saying "I am enough just as I am." This practice helps to shift the focus from negative self-talk to positive self-talk, which can improve self-esteem and reduce stress and anxiety.

Practicing gratitude is another technique for developing positive self-talk. Focusing on what you are grateful for can help shift your mindset towards positivity and improve your self-talk. Take time each day to think of things you are thankful for and express gratitude. This practice can help promote a more positive outlook on life and increase feelings of well-being. For example, instead of focusing on what we lack or what went wrong in our day, we can make a conscious effort to think about the things we are grateful for, such as our health, our loved ones, or the opportunities we have. This can help us reframe our thoughts towards positivity and foster a more optimistic mindset.

Using positive affirmations is another powerful technique for developing positive self-talk. Positive affirmations are statements that affirm positive qualities about oneself. Repeat these affirmations to yourself regularly, such as "I am worthy of love and respect" or "I am capable of achieving my goals." This practice can help to reinforce positive beliefs and improve self-esteem.

We can state five positive affirmations about today.

1. Today is full of opportunities and possibilities.
2. I am capable and worthy of achieving my goals today.
3. I choose to approach each challenge today with a positive mindset.
4. I am grateful for everything that today will bring.
5. Today, I will prioritize self-care and self-love.

Finally, visualizing success is a technique for developing positive self-talk that can help build confidence and belief in oneself. Visualization involves creating a mental image of success and achievement. Visualize yourself achieving your goals and succeeding in what you set out to do. This practice can help to develop a more positive mindset and promote resilience in the face of challenges. For example, if someone is preparing for a job interview, they can visualize themselves walking into the interview room feeling confident, answering questions articulately and with ease, and ultimately receiving a job offer. By focusing on positive outcomes and building a mental picture of success, individuals can develop a more positive and confident mindset, which can help them to achieve their goals.

Various techniques can be utilized to develop positive self-talk, such as reframing negative thoughts, practicing gratitude, using positive affirmations, and visualizing success. The intentional cultivation of positive self-talk can lead to an improvement in our mental and emotional well-being, as well as the reduction of stress and anxiety, and an increase in resilience when facing challenges. These techniques can easily be integrated into our daily routine and have a significant impact on our overall well-being.

3.3 The Role of Affirmations and Visualizations in Positive Self-talk

Affirmations and visualizations are powerful tools for developing positive self-talk. Affirmations are positive statements that are repeated to oneself, reinforcing positive qualities and strengths within oneself. For example, an affirmation might be "I am confident and capable in everything that I do." This affirmation reinforces the belief in oneself and promotes a positive self-image. Affirmations are a way to consciously choose and focus on positive self-talk, rather than allowing negative self-talk to dominate one's thoughts and feelings.

Here's a joke for you: Why did the positive affirmation cross the road? To get to the bright side!

Visualizations are another tool for developing positive self-talk. Visualization involves creating a mental image of success and achievement. By visualizing oneself achieving a goal, such as giving a successful presentation or completing a challenging task, one can develop a sense of confidence and belief in oneself. Visualization helps to create a positive mindset and outlook, which can lead to improved self-talk and overall well-being. Imagine you're giving a big presentation in front of a large audience, and you start to feel nervous and doubtful about your abilities. Suddenly, you visualize yourself as a superhero with a cape, soaring through the air with confidence and ease. You imagine your audience cheering you on as you deliver your presentation flawlessly, with a big smile on your face. As you land back on the ground, you feel empowered and energized, ready to tackle any challenge that comes your way. This visualization helps to shift your mindset from doubt to confidence, and reminds you that you have the power within you to succeed.

When practiced consistently, affirmations and visualizations can become ingrained in one's thinking and self-talk. Over time, this can lead to a more positive mindset and outlook on life, as well as improved self-esteem and confidence. By consciously choosing to focus on positive self-talk, one can begin to shift away from negative self-talk and develop a more optimistic and solution-focused mindset.

In conclusion, affirmations and visualizations play a key role in developing positive self-talk. By reinforcing positive qualities and strengths within oneself, affirmations can promote a more positive self-image and outlook on life. Visualization helps to create a mental image of success and achievement, which can lead to improved confidence and belief in oneself. When practiced consistently, affirmations and visualizations can become ingrained in one's thinking and self-talk, promoting a more positive mindset and overall well-being.

Positive self-talk is a valuable tool for improving mental and emotional well-being. Utilizing techniques such as reframing negative thoughts, practicing gratitude, using positive affirmations, and visualizing success can promote a more positive outlook on life and help develop positive self-talk. Through cultivating positive self-talk, individuals can boost their self-esteem, reduce stress and anxiety, and build resilience to overcome challenges.

Self-talk Affirmations

These affirmations are recommended to be read early in the morning, afternoon, and evening to maximize their impact.

There are times when I struggle to believe in myself and my abilities. During these moments, it can be easy to fall into negative self-talk and doubt my own worth. But it's important for me to remember that I am unique and valuable, just as I am. I have a purpose and a mission in this world that only I can fulfill.

When I'm feeling uncertain, it can be helpful to remind myself of my strengths and potential. I can say to myself, "I am proud of myself and all that I have accomplished. I am capable of achieving great things." These positive affirmations can give me a much-needed boost of confidence and motivation to keep pushing forward towards my goals.

I must also remember that my worth is not determined by my achievements or my mistakes. I am loved and cherished beyond measure, simply for being who I am. I have a divine spark within me that shines brightly, and this inherent value cannot be diminished by external circumstances.

I know that I will face challenges and obstacles along the way, but I have the strength and resilience to overcome them. I am not alone in my struggles, and I have people in my life who guide and support me through every step.

My imperfections are what make me beautiful and unique. It's important for me to embrace my flaws and celebrate my strengths, rather than trying to conform to society's expectations of perfection. I am deserving of love and respect, and I should never let anyone else's words or actions make me doubt my worth.

I should never be afraid to dream big and pursue my passions. I have the creativity and courage to make my dreams a reality. And if I make mistakes along the way, I am forgiven and worthy of grace and mercy.

Above all, I must remember that I am enough, just as I am. I should embrace my true self and know that I am loved unconditionally. These loving words, spoken to me as if from a higher power, can inspire me to believe in myself and my potential to make a positive impact in the world.

4

Embracing Your Imperfections

4.1 Understanding that Imperfection is a Natural part of the Human Experience

E mbracing one's imperfections is an important part of cultivating self-love and building a positive relationship with oneself. Imperfection is a natural part of the human experience, yet we often hold ourselves to unrealistic standards of perfection. In this chapter, we will explore strategies for accepting and embracing our flaws, and the power of self-compassion in cultivating self-love.

4.2 Strategies for Accepting and Embracing your Flaws

It's important to recognize that everyone has imperfections and flaws, and that it's okay to make mistakes. Striving for perfection can lead to feelings of stress and anxiety, and can prevent us from fully enjoying our experiences. Accepting our imperfections and embracing our flaws can help us to feel more comfortable in our own skin, and allow us to focus on what really matters in life.

One strategy for accepting and embracing our flaws is to practice self-compassion. Self-compassion involves treating ourselves with kindness, understanding, and acceptance. When we make a mistake or fall short of our expectations, we can offer ourselves the same compassion that we would offer to a friend. This can help to reduce negative self-talk and increase our self-esteem. One example of practicing self-compassion to accept and embrace our flaws is to speak to ourselves with kindness and understanding, just as we would to a friend. For instance, if we make a mistake or fail at something, instead of berating ourselves and calling ourselves names, we can offer ourselves words of comfort and encouragement, such as "it's okay, I'm only human and I'm doing my best." This approach helps us to be more gentle and forgiving towards ourselves, and allows us to recognize that making mistakes and having flaws is a natural part of being human.

Another strategy is to reframe our negative thoughts about ourselves. Instead of focusing on our flaws and shortcomings, we can focus on our strengths and positive qualities. For example, if we're feeling self-conscious about a physical imperfection, we can remind ourselves of our other positive qualities, such as our sense of humor or our kindness.

It can also be helpful to practice self-care and engage in activities that make us feel good about ourselves. This can include exercise, spending time in nature, or pursuing hobbies and interests that we enjoy. Taking care of ourselves can help us to feel more confident and comfortable in our own skin.

Ultimately, embracing our imperfections is about accepting ourselves for who we are, flaws and all. It's about recognizing that we are all imperfect, and that this is what makes us human. By practicing self-compassion and focusing on our positive qualities, we can cultivate self-love and build a positive relationship with ourselves.

There are several exercises one can do to embrace their imperfections and build a more positive relationship with themselves.

Here are a few examples:

1. Make a list of your flaws:

   Acknowledge your flaws, write them down, and understand that they are a natural part of the human experience. Instead of fighting against them, learn to accept and embrace them.

2. Practice self-compassion:

   Be kind to yourself, as you would to a friend. Treat yourself with love, respect, and understanding, even when you make mistakes or experience setbacks.

3. Reframe negative self-talk:

   Challenge your negative self-talk by asking yourself if it's really true, or if there's another, more positive way to look at the situation.

4. Celebrate your successes:

   Recognize and celebrate your achievements, no matter how small they may seem. This can help boost your self-esteem and remind you of your strengths.

4.3 The Power of Self-compassion in Cultivating Self-love

Embracing your imperfections is an essential step towards culti-vating self-love and building a positive relationship with yourself. But how do you go about doing that? Here are some exercises and strategies that you can practice to embrace your imperfections and increase self-acceptance.

One of the most important things you can do is to practice self-compassion. When negative self-talk arises, try speaking to yourself as you would to a good friend. Ask yourself what you need in that moment, and offer yourself kind and supportive words. Recognize that you are human and imperfect, and that it's okay to make mistakes.

Focusing on your positive qualities is another helpful exercise. Take some time to reflect on your positive qualities, skills, and accomplishments. Make a list of them and read them to yourself regularly. This can help to counterbalance any negative self-talk and increase self-esteem.

Reframing negative thoughts is also key to embracing your imper-fections. When negative thoughts arise, try reframing them into more positive and constructive self-talk. For example, instead of saying "I'm not good enough," try saying "I am enough just as I am, and I can continue to grow and learn."

Practicing self-care is another important exercise. Engage in ac-tivities that make you feel good about yourself, such as exercise, spending time with loved ones, or pursuing hobbies and interests that bring you joy. This can help to boost self-esteem and confi-dence.

Embracing vulnerability is another important step towards em-bracing your imperfections. Recognize that vulnerability is a natural part of the human experience, and that it's okay to ask for help or admit when you need support. Embracing vulnerabili-ty can help to foster deeper connections with others and build a more positive relationship with yourself.

Finally, it's important to practice self-forgiveness. If you're holding onto past mistakes or regrets, try offering yourself the same compassion and forgiveness that you would offer to a loved one. Recognize that you are human and imperfect, and that making mistakes is a natural part of the learning process. For example, if you're feeling overwhelmed by a project at work, instead of trying to hide your struggles and pretending that everything is fine, you could reach out to a trusted colleague or mentor for support and guidance. By embracing your vulnerability and seeking help when you need it, you can learn and grow from your experiences, and ultimately become more resilient and confident in yourself. Because embracing vulnerability involves acknowledging and accepting the reality that everyone has flaws and makes mistakes, and being willing to share that with others. It can help build stronger connections and relationships, as it allows others to see and relate to the real, authentic parts of ourselves.

By practicing these exercises and others like them, you can learn to embrace your imperfections and build a more positive and loving relationship with yourself. Remember that you are unique and valuable, flaws and all, and that your imperfections are what make you beautifully human.

Self-talk to Embrace One's Imperfections

As I reflect on my imperfections, I remind myself that I am wonderfully and fearfully made, flaws and all. My imperfections do not diminish my worth, they make me unique and special in my own way. I love myself just the way I am, knowing that I do not need to change or be perfect to be loved and accepted by myself.

As I face struggles and pain, I remind myself that I am not alone in my imperfections. I have the power to help myself through them, knowing that I am capable of growth and learning. I embrace my imperfections and let them be a part of my journey.

I will not let my imperfections define me or hold me back from my dreams. I know that I am capable of achieving anything I set my mind to, flaws and all. My imperfections make me relatable and approachable to others, giving me the ability to connect with people on a deeper level and make a difference in their lives.

As I offer myself kindness and compassion, just as God offers it to me, I remind myself that my imperfections are a reminder that I am human, and that is a beautiful thing. I embrace my humanity and all that makes me who I am, knowing that I am worthy of love and acceptance just as I am.

5

Letting Go of Self-Doubt

In this chapter, we will explore the topic of self-doubt and how it can hold us back from living our best lives. Self-doubt is a common experience that can arise when we are faced with challenges, uncertainty, or fear of failure. It can manifest as negative self-talk, perfectionism, and imposter syndrome. However, letting go of self-doubt is essential to building confidence and pursuing our goals and dreams.

To let go of self-doubt, it's important to first recognize when it is present. Negative self-talk, avoidance behaviors, and feelings of anxiety or overwhelm can all be signs of self-doubt. Once we have identified these patterns, we can begin to take action to overcome them.

One strategy for letting go of self-doubt is to challenge our negative thoughts and beliefs. We can do this by asking ourselves if our thoughts are based on facts or assumptions, and by considering alternative perspectives. It's also helpful to focus on our strengths and accomplishments, rather than our weaknesses or perceived failures. One example of challenging negative thoughts and beliefs to let go of self-doubt is by identifying and questioning the evidence supporting these thoughts. For instance, if you have a negative thought like "I'm not good enough," you can ask yourself if there is any evidence to support this belief. Then, you can look for evidence that contradicts this belief and focus on that instead. This process of questioning and reframing negative thoughts can help you overcome self-doubt and cultivate a more positive mindset.

Another strategy is to take action, even if we feel uncertain or afraid. By facing our fears and taking small steps towards our goals, we can build confidence and overcome self-doubt. It's also important to celebrate our successes, no matter how small, and to acknowledge our progress along the way.

Practicing self-compassion is another key element in letting go of self-doubt. It's important to be kind and understanding towards ourselves, recognizing that we are all human and imperfect. We can offer ourselves the same compassion and support that we would offer to a loved one. One key point to remember when practicing self-compassion in letting go of self-doubt is to treat yourself with the same kindness and understanding that you would offer to a close friend who is struggling. This means acknowledging that everyone makes mistakes and experiences setbacks, and recognizing that these experiences do not define our worth or value as a person. By offering ourselves compassion and understanding, we can let go of self-doubt and move forward with greater confidence and self-assurance.

Releasing self-doubt necessitates a dedication to our personal growth and progress. We can conquer self-doubt and lead a fulfilling life by acknowledging our worth, confronting our pessimistic thoughts, taking action, and practicing self-compassion.

5.1 Understanding the Root Causes of Self-doubt

Self-doubt can be a significant obstacle in developing self-love and achieving personal growth. Understanding the root causes of self-doubt can help us to overcome it and develop a more positive and self-affirming mindset.

One of the primary causes of self-doubt is negative past experiences. Trauma, rejection, or failure can all contribute to feelings of self-doubt, as we may believe that we are not good enough or that we will fail again. Negative past experiences can be a primary cause of self-doubt, often leading to an inability to forgive oneself. Forgiveness is a personal and individual process that requires self-reflection and introspection. It may be helpful to seek guidance from a trusted friend, family member, or therapist in working through past events and practicing self-forgiveness. These negative experiences can create a pattern of self-doubt that is difficult to break without self-awareness and self-compassion.

Another cause of self-doubt is perfectionism. When we hold ourselves to impossibly high standards, we set ourselves up for failure and disappointment. This can lead to feelings of inadequacy and self-doubt, as we may believe that we are not good enough unless we are perfect. An example of how perfectionism can lead to self-doubt is a student who sets unrealistic expectations for themselves in school. They may believe that they need to get straight A's in every class to be successful and feel good about themselves. When they inevitably receive a lower grade or struggle in a class, they may feel like a failure and experience self-doubt. This negative self-talk can then lead to a lack of motivation and a further decline in academic performance, creating a cycle of self-doubt and low self-esteem.

Social comparison is also a significant contributor to self-doubt. When we compare ourselves to others, we may feel that we do not measure up or that we are inferior in some way. This can be especially true in the age of social media, where we are constantly bombarded with images and stories of people who appear to have perfect lives. We may compare ourselves to their highlight reels and feel like we don't measure up. An example could be scrolling through Instagram and seeing pictures of your friends on lavish vacations or posting about their successful careers, which can lead to feelings of self-doubt and insecurity about your own life. This can lead to feelings of self-doubt and inadequacy.

Finally, self-doubt can also be caused by negative self-talk. When we engage in self-criticism and negative self-talk, we reinforce our doubts and insecurities, making it difficult to develop self-love and confidence. One way to prevent engaging in self-criticism and negative self-talk is to practice self-compassion. Instead of beating ourselves up over our mistakes and flaws, we can approach ourselves with kindness and understanding. For example, if we make a mistake, we can remind ourselves that everyone makes mistakes and it doesn't define our worth as a person. We can then offer ourselves words of encouragement and support, as we would a close friend who is going through a tough time. This can help to shift our mindset towards self-acceptance and build a more positive relationship with ourselves.

5.2 The Dangers of Self-doubt on Self-esteem and Self-love

Self-doubt can be incredibly damaging to one's self-esteem and self-love. When we doubt ourselves, we may constantly second-guess our decisions and abilities, leading to a lack of confidence and a negative self-image. This can prevent us from pursuing our goals and taking risks, ultimately limiting our potential for personal growth and fulfillment. Self-doubt can also lead to a cycle of negative self-talk and self-criticism, which can erode our self-esteem and sense of self-worth. When we constantly tell ourselves that we are not good enough or capable enough, we begin to internalize these beliefs and they become a self-fulfilling prophecy.

It can cause us to seek validation and approval from others, rather than trusting in our own abilities and intuition. This can lead to a dependence on external validation, making us vulnerable to criticism and rejection.

Ultimately, self-doubt can be a major obstacle in the journey towards self-love and self-acceptance. Self-love and self-acceptance can be compared to a seed and a tree. Just as a seed needs to be nurtured and cared for in order to grow into a strong and healthy tree, self-love and self-acceptance require intentional effort and self-care in order to flourish. Just as a tree must accept and adapt to its surroundings to thrive, we must accept and embrace all parts of ourselves, including our flaws and imperfections, in order to fully love and accept ourselves. And just as a tree provides shade, shelter, and nourishment to others, when we practice self-love and self-acceptance, we can radiate positivity and inspire those around us to do the same. It is important to recognize and address the root causes of self-doubt in order to overcome it and cultivate a positive relationship with oneself.

5.3 Techniques for Overcoming Self-doubt and Cultivating Confidence

Self-doubt is a common experience that can hold us back from reaching our full potential and achieving our goals. Fortunately, there are several techniques that we can use to overcome self-doubt and cultivate confidence.

One effective technique is to challenge negative self-talk. Negative thoughts and beliefs can contribute to self-doubt, so it's important to identify them and challenge their validity. We can do this by looking for evidence that contradicts our negative thoughts and replacing them with positive affirmations.

Another technique is to celebrate our successes. Taking time to reflect on our accomplishments, no matter how small they may seem, can help boost our confidence and remind us of our capabilities. We can also focus on our strengths and positive qualities by making a list and reading it regularly. Celebrating our successes is an important aspect of personal growth and development. There are many ways to celebrate our successes, including treating ourselves to something special, sharing our success with others, taking time to reflect on our accomplishments, writing down our successes, and setting new goals. Treating ourselves to something special is a great way to celebrate our successes. This could be something as simple as enjoying a nice meal or indulging in a spa day. It could also be a more significant event, such as a shopping trip or a vacation. The key is to do something that we enjoy and that makes us feel good. Sharing our success with others is another important way to celebrate. This could involve telling our friends and family about our accomplishments, or it could involve throwing a party or gathering to celebrate with others. Sharing our success with others can help us feel validated and supported, and can provide us with the motivation we need to continue on our path. Taking time to reflect on our success and what we did to achieve it is also important. This can help us feel more confident and motivated to continue on our path. We can reflect on the skills and strengths that we used to achieve our success, and we can think about how we can apply these skills and strengths in the future.

Writing down our success and how it makes us feel can serve as a reminder of our achievement and help us stay focused on our goals. We can keep a journal or notebook where we record our successes and how they make us feel. This can be a powerful tool for building self-confidence and self-esteem.

Taking action is another effective technique for overcoming self-doubt. Setting small goals and taking steps towards achieving them can help build momentum and boost confidence. Even small successes can be powerful in building confidence and overcoming self-doubt. An example of taking action to overcome self-doubt could be signing up for a class or workshop to develop a new skill. Let's say someone has always wanted to learn how to paint but has never tried it because they don't believe they have any artistic talent. By taking action and signing up for a painting class, they are challenging their self-doubt and giving themselves an opportunity to learn and grow. As they start to paint and see progress, their self-doubt may start to fade away, and they may even discover a newfound passion for painting. The act of taking action, even in the face of self-doubt, can be empowering and help us build confidence in ourselves and our abilities.

Engaging in self-care is a crucial aspect of building confidence and overcoming self-doubt. By partaking in activities that bring us pleasure, such as exercise, spending time with loved ones, or pursuing hobbies and interests that make us happy, we can boost our self-esteem and feel more competent. In conclusion, self-doubt can be a barrier to our success and happiness. However, by employing techniques like challenging negative self-talk, celebrating our achievements, focusing on our strengths, taking action, and prioritizing self-care, we can overcome self-doubt and develop confidence. By cultivating confidence, we can achieve our objectives and lead a more satisfying and fulfilling life.

Self talk Letting Go of Self-doubt

As a person, I am capable of so much more than I realize. I will not let my doubts and fears hold me back from achieving my dreams.

God has given me unique gifts and talents that are meant to be shared with the world. I will embrace them and have confidence in my abilities.

I will not compare myself to others, for I am fearfully and wonderfully made. I am exactly who I am meant to be, and that is enough.

God is with me always, guiding and supporting me through every challenge and triumph. I am never alone in my self-doubt.

I will believe in myself and trust in the plan that God has for my life. I know that He is leading me towards my purpose and my destiny.

I am loved unconditionally, flaws and all. My worth is not determined by my successes or failures, but by the inherent value that I possess as God's beloved creation.

I will let go of my self-doubt and have faith in the journey that lies ahead. I know that God is walking beside me every step of the way.

I have a unique purpose and mission in this world that only I can fulfill. I will trust in the strength and resilience that God has placed within me to accomplish all that I am meant to do.

I will not be afraid to take risks and pursue my passions. I have everything I need within me to succeed and thrive.

6

Celebrating Your Strengths

In Chapter 6, we will explore the importance of celebrating our strengths and how it can positively impact our self-esteem and overall well-being. We will discuss ways to identify our strengths and practical strategies for incorporating them into our daily lives.

Understanding the significance of celebrating our strengths involves acknowledging our positive qualities, skills, and abilities. By focusing on our strengths, we can boost our self-esteem and confidence, leading to greater motivation and productivity.

Identifying our strengths can be challenging, especially if we are used to being self-critical. However, there are several strategies that can help us discover our strengths, such as reflecting on past accomplishments, seeking feedback from others, and experimenting with new activities and hobbies.

One way to identify our strengths is to ask for feedback from people we trust and respect. This could be friends, family members, colleagues, or even a mentor. Ask them what they think your strengths are and what you do well. You may be surprised by what they say, and it can be a helpful exercise to see yourself from someone else's perspective.

Another way to identify your strengths is to think about what comes naturally to you, what you enjoy doing, and what you feel confident in. Reflect on times when you have achieved success, and think about what skills and abilities you used to make that happen.

You can also take a strengths assessment test, such as the CliftonStrengths assessment or the VIA Character Strengths survey. These tests are designed to identify your natural talents and help you understand how to use them to achieve your goals.

An example of how to identify your strengths using feedback from others:

Let's say you are trying to identify your strengths for a job interview. You can reach out to previous colleagues, supervisors, or mentors and ask them to provide you with feedback on what they think your strengths are.

For example, you might ask them:

1. What do you think are my top three strengths?
2. What did you notice that I did particularly well when we worked together?
3. What would you say is my biggest contribution to the team/project/company?

By asking these questions, you can gain insight into how others perceive your strengths and get a sense of what you excel at in the workplace. Based on their feedback, you can then prepare to talk about these strengths in your job interview and give concrete examples of how you have used them to achieve success in the past.

Lastly, try to shift your focus from self-criticism to self-compassion. Acknowledge your successes and celebrate your strengths, no matter how small they may seem. By focusing on what you do well, you can build your confidence and feel more empowered to tackle challenges in the future.

Once we have identified our strengths, it's important to incorporate them into our daily lives. This can be done through setting goals that align with our strengths, seeking out opportunities that allow us to use our strengths, and expressing gratitude for our strengths and accomplishments.

By celebrating our strengths, we can also learn to appreciate the strengths of others, fostering deeper connections and relationships. It's important to remember that everyone has unique strengths and abilities, and we can all learn from each other.

6.1 Recognizing your Unique Strengths and Talents

Recognizing your unique strengths and talents is a critical step in celebrating your abilities and building self-confidence. Often, we may focus more on our weaknesses or areas of improvement, leading to feelings of inadequacy and self-doubt. However, by shifting our focus towards our strengths, we can learn to appreciate and celebrate our unique abilities.

One way to recognize your talents/strengths is to reflect on past successes and accomplishments. Think about times when you felt proud of yourself, and consider what skills and strengths you used to achieve those successes. You can also ask for feedback from trusted friends or family members, or take a personality or strengths assessment to gain a better understanding of your unique abilities.

It's important to remember that everyone has their own set of strengths and talents, and there is no "right" or "wrong" way to be. By embracing and celebrating your strengths, you can learn to appreciate your individuality and build self-confidence.

Celebrating your strengths can also help you to achieve your goals and pursue your passions. By recognizing the strengths you possess, you can leverage them to overcome challenges and achieve success. For example, if you are a good communicator, you can use this strength to build relationships and collaborate effectively with others.

Recognizing and celebrating your strengths is an important aspect of building self-confidence and cultivating self-love. By focusing on your unique abilities and appreciating what makes you special, you can learn to embrace your individuality and live a more fulfilling life.

6.2 Strategies for Leveraging your Strengths to Boost Self-love

Embracing and celebrating your strengths is an important part of cultivating self-love and acceptance. By identifying your unique talents and abilities, you can begin to appreciate the qualities that make you special and valuable.

To begin, it's important to take some time to reflect on your strengths. Consider what activities come naturally to you, what you enjoy doing, and what others have complimented you on in the past. Make a list of these strengths and refer back to it regularly as a reminder of your unique qualities.

Once you have identified your strengths, it's important to fully embrace them. Celebrate your talents and acknowledge the things that make you who you are. Don't shy away from your strengths, but rather, lean into them and allow them to shine.

In addition to embracing your strengths, it's important to focus on them as well. Rather than dwelling on your weaknesses or areas of struggle, focus on your strengths and put them to work in your daily life. Whether it's at work, in your hobbies, or in your relationships, use your strengths to make a positive impact and achieve your goals.

Moreover, it's important to leverage your strengths to achieve your goals and pursue your passions. When faced with obstacles or challenges, use your strengths to help you overcome them and achieve success. By doing so, you can build confidence and self-love through your accomplishments.

Finally, sharing your strengths with others can also be a powerful way to boost self-love and build positive relationships. Offer your unique talents and skills to help others, whether it's through volunteering or simply sharing your knowledge and expertise. By doing so, you not only benefit others but also reinforce your own value and worth.

To sum up, it is crucial to identify, accept, and utilize your strengths to develop self-love and self-acceptance. When you concentrate on your distinctive abilities and apply them in your life, you can attain success, increase your self-assurance, and improve your interpersonal connections.

6.3 The Importance of Self-appreciation in Cultivating Positive Self-talk

Self-appreciation is a vital aspect of cultivating positive self-talk. Appreciating oneself means acknowledging and valuing one's own positive qualities, achievements, and abilities. When one appreciates oneself, it creates a positive self-image, self-worth, and self-esteem.

Self-appreciation is essential for cultivating positive self-talk because it helps to counteract negative self-talk. Negative self-talk can be damaging to one's mental and emotional health, leading to low self-esteem, self-doubt, and anxiety. By cultivating self-appreciation, one can counteract these negative thoughts and replace them with positive affirmations and self-talk.

One way to cultivate self-appreciation and counteract negative self-talk is to practice self-affirmations. Self-affirmations are positive statements that you can repeat to yourself to help build a positive self-image and promote self-appreciation.

For example, you can write down or say to yourself affirmations such as:

1. I am worthy of love and respect.
2. I am capable of achieving my goals.
3. I am proud of myself for [insert something you have ac complished.
4. I am confident in my abilities.
5. I am grateful for my strengths and weaknesses.

By regularly practicing self-affirmations, you can reprogram your negative self-talk into positive self-talk and develop a more compassionate and accepting relationship with yourself. Additionally, focusing on your strengths and accomplishments can help you to recognize your worth and build self-confidence.

Self-appreciation also helps to build resilience in the face of challenges and setbacks. When one appreciates their strengths and accomplishments, they are better equipped to navigate difficult situations and bounce back from setbacks. This positive mindset helps to build self-confidence and can lead to greater success in all areas of life.

Self-appreciation promotes a more positive outlook on life. It helps to cultivate a sense of gratitude and contentment, allowing one to focus on the positive aspects of life rather than dwelling on the negative.

I always remind myself that self-appreciation is essential for cultivating a positive outlook on life. By appreciating myself, I am creating a more fulfilling life for myself. When I value myself, I attract positivity and abundance into my life. I understand that practicing self-appreciation helps me to see the good in myself and in others. When I appreciate my strengths and accomplishments, I am better able to handle challenges and setbacks. By practicing self-appreciation, I am cultivating a deeper sense of self-love and self-acceptance within myself. I am committed to regularly reminding myself of the importance of self-appreciation and using positive affirmations to reinforce this mindset.

I acknowledge that self-appreciation is essential for cultivating positive self-talk. It helps me to counteract negative self-talk, build resilience, and promote a more positive outlook on life. By cultivating self-appreciation, I can create a positive self-image and increase my self-worth, leading to greater mental and emotional well-being. I commit to regularly practicing self-affirmations, celebrating my strengths, and appreciating my accomplishments. By doing so, I am developing a more compassionate and accepting relationship with myself, which will help me to navigate life's challenges with greater ease and positivity. I conclude this chapter with self talk, this is something you should read first thing in the morning to improve your outlook in life.

Self-talk to Celebrate ones Strength

I am so proud of the unique gifts and talents that I possess. I am a precious creation, and my strengths make me shine. I know that I have so much to offer the world with my strengths, and I embrace them fully. By sharing them with others, I can make a positive impact on the world around me.

I believe that my strengths are a reflection of God's love for me. I know that I am fearfully and wonderfully made, and my strengths are part of what makes me so special. They are not just skills or abilities, they are part of who I am. I celebrate them and use them to bring joy and light into the world.

I see my strengths and the potential within me to achieve great things. I believe in myself and trust in the strengths that God has given me. I know that I am not defined by my weaknesses, but by my strengths. I celebrate them and let them shine, for they are a reflection of the divine within me.

I treasure and appreciate my strengths as a gift from God. I take time to honor and celebrate them, and I remember that they make me who I am. I am grateful for the unique qualities that make me who I am, and I know that with my strengths, I can accomplish anything I set my mind to.

7

Building a Supportive Self-Talk Environment

7.1 The Role of Environment in Shaping Self-talk

The environment in which we live, work, and interact with others can have a significant impact on the way we talk to ourselves. Our environment can either support or hinder our efforts to cultivate positive self-talk. Negative or toxic environments can lead to negative self-talk, while positive and supportive environments can foster a more positive inner dialogue.

Negative environments can include places where there is a lot of criticism, judgment, or negativity. For example, a workplace where there is constant competition and comparison can contribute to feelings of inadequacy and self-doubt. Similarly, relationships that are emotionally abusive or manipulative can contribute to negative self-talk, as the person may internalize the negative messages they receive from others.

On the other hand, positive and supportive environments can help to build a more positive inner dialogue. This can include environments where there is encouragement, support, and affirmation. For example, a workplace that values collaboration and recognizes individual contributions can help to build confidence and self-esteem. Similarly, relationships that are built on love, respect, and healthy communication can promote positive self-talk and a sense of self-worth.

It's important to recognize that we have some control over our environment and can take steps to create a more supportive and positive space. This can include surrounding ourselves with positive influences, such as supportive friends and family members, engaging in activities that bring us joy and fulfillment, and seeking out positive and uplifting media and literature.

Our self-talk can be shaped by the environment we live in and the people we interact with. To foster a positive inner dialogue and develop a stronger sense of self-worth, it is important to cultivate a positive and supportive environment. By surrounding ourselves with positivity, we can work towards building a more optimistic outlook on life and a healthier relationship with ourselves.

7.2 Strategies for Creating a Supportive Self-talk Environment

Building a supportive self-talk environment is essential for promoting positive self-talk and cultivating a more positive mindset.

Here are some strategies to create a supportive self-talk environment:

First, surround yourself with positive influences. Spend time with people who support and encourage you, and limit your exposure to negative influences. Negative self-talk, negative news, and social media that triggers negative emotions can all contribute to a negative mindset.

Secondly, create positive affirmations. Make a list of positive affirmations that reflect your values, goals, and strengths.

Some examples of positive affirmations:

1. I am kind, compassionate, and always willing to help others.
2. I am committed to living with integrity and honesty in all areas of my life.
3. I am dedicated to achieving my goals and making my dreams a reality.
4. I am proud of my strengths and abilities, and I use them to make a positive impact in the world.
5. I am focused on taking care of my physical and mental health, and I prioritize self-care.
6. I am a creative and innovative thinker, and I approach challenges with curiosity and openness.

Repeat them to yourself regularly and post them in visible places, such as on your mirror or computer screen. This can help to counteract any negative self-talk and promote more positive self-talk.

Thirdly, use positive language when speaking to yourself and others. Avoid negative self-talk and replace it with positive affirmations and constructive feedback. When we use positive language, we shift our focus to the positive aspects of our lives and create a more optimistic and hopeful mindset.

Instead of saying "I'm not good at this," you can say "I'm still learning, and I'll get better with practice." This positive language acknowledges the current struggle but reframes it as an opportunity for growth and improvement.

Another example is instead of saying "I'm so stressed out," you can say "I'm feeling challenged right now, but I'm capable of handling it." This positive language acknowledges the difficulty of the situation but emphasizes your ability to cope with it.

When speaking to others, you can use positive language by offering compliments and encouragement. For example, instead of saying "That's not how you do it," you can say "That's a great start! Have you considered trying it this way?" This positive language acknowledges their effort and offers helpful suggestions for improvement.

Using positive language can help to create a more supportive and empowering environment, both for yourself and for others.

Fourthly, practice self-compassion. Treat yourself with kindness and compassion, just as you would treat a good friend. When negative self-talk arises, offer yourself kind and supportive words, and recognize that mistakes and setbacks are a natural part of the learning and growing process.

Finally, engage in self-care. Take care of your physical, emotional, and mental well-being by engaging in activities that promote self-care. This can include exercise, meditation, journaling, or spending time with loved ones. When we prioritize self-care, we are better equipped to manage stress and promote positive self-talk.

7.3 Surrounding Yourself with Positive People who Uplift and Encourage you

Surrounding yourself with positive people who uplift and encourage you is a powerful way to create a supportive self-talk environment. When you spend time with people who are positive and supportive, you are more likely to adopt their optimistic mindset and positive self-talk patterns.

To create a supportive social circle, start by identifying the people in your life who consistently uplift and encourage you. Spend more time with these individuals and nurture those relationships. You can also seek out new social connections through clubs, classes, or community groups that align with your interests and values.

It's also important to set healthy boundaries with people who consistently engage in negative self-talk or bring you down. While it's important to offer compassion and support to those who may be struggling, you do not have to tolerate constant negativity or harmful behavior.

In addition to building positive relationships, you can also create a supportive self-talk environment by being mindful of the language you use with yourself and others. Practice positive self-talk by affirming your strengths and progress, and avoid harsh self-criticism or negative self-talk.

Creating a supportive self-talk environment involves positive influences, healthy relationships, and a compassionate mindset towards yourself and others.

Self-talk to Cultivate a Positive Mindset

Words to tell yourself in the morning, afternoon, and night.

I am wonderfully and fearfully made, with unique strengths and talents that I can use to make a positive impact in the world. I do not need to compare myself to others, for I am fearfully and wonderfully made just as I am. I can embrace my imperfections and use them as opportunities for growth and learning.

I am capable of achieving great things, and I do not need to let my doubts and fears hold me back. I have been given unique gifts and talents that are meant to be shared with the world, and I can trust in the plan that has been laid out for me.

I am worthy of love and respect, and I do not need to let anyone else's words or actions make me doubt my worth. I can be kind to myself, just as my creator is kind to me, and offer myself the same love and compassion that I would offer to a loved one.

I have a divine spark within me that shines brightly. I can believe in myself and trust in the power of my own potential. I can let go of my self-doubt and have faith in the journey that lies ahead. I am never alone in my struggles, for my creator is always with me, guiding and supporting me through every challenge and triumph.

8
Self-Love in Practice

In this chapter, we explore practical ways to cultivate self-love in our daily lives. Self-love is a journey that requires consistent effort and practice, but the benefits are immeasurable. When we love ourselves, we are better equipped to handle challenges, build meaningful relationships, and pursue our dreams with confidence.

One of the most important ways to practice self-love is to prioritize our own needs and well-being. This means taking care of ourselves physically, emotionally, and mentally. Some strategies for practicing self-care include getting enough sleep, eating nourishing foods, engaging in regular exercise, and taking time for relaxation and leisure activities.

Another important aspect of self-love is setting healthy boundaries. This means saying no to things that do not serve our well-being and setting limits on how much time and energy we give to others. It also means treating ourselves with kindness and respect, and not tolerating mistreatment from others.

Practicing gratitude is another powerful way to cultivate self-love. When we focus on the things we are thankful for, we shift our attention away from our perceived shortcomings and appreciate the abundance in our lives. This can help us develop a more positive mindset and increase our overall sense of well-being.

Learning to accept ourselves, flaws and all, is another key component of self-love. Instead of criticizing ourselves for our perceived shortcomings, we can practice self-compassion and offer ourselves the same love and kindness we would offer a dear friend.

Ultimately, practicing self-love is about treating ourselves with the same love and care that we would give to someone we love deeply. By prioritizing our own needs and well-being, setting healthy boundaries, cultivating gratitude, and practicing self-acceptance, we can build a strong foundation of self-love that will support us throughout our lives.

8.1 Putting Positive Self-talk into Practice

Practicing positive self-talk is a powerful way to cultivate self-love and boost self-esteem. However, it can be challenging to put into practice if you're not used to speaking kindly to yourself.

Here are some strategies to help you start incorporating positive self-talk into your daily routine.

1. Start small:

   Don't feel like you have to completely change your self-talk all at once. Begin by practicing positive self-talk in small ways, such as complimenting yourself for a job well done or offering yourself words of encouragement during a challenging moment. Gradually build on these positive moments to form a more consistent habit.

2. Be consistent:

   Consistency is key when it comes to building a new habit. Set aside time each day to practice positive self-talk, whether it's in the morning, before bed, or throughout the day. Make it a non-negotiable part of your routine to help it become a natural part of your thought process.

3. Use visual cues:

Post positive affirmations or reminders in visible places, such as on your mirror or computer screen, to help you stay mindful of your self-talk throughout the day. These visual cues can serve as a powerful reminder to be kind to yourself.

4. Monitor your self-talk:

Pay attention to your self-talk throughout the day, and notice when negative thoughts arise. Challenge these thoughts by reframing them into positive affirmations or constructive feedback. For example, instead of saying "I'm such an idiot," try saying "I made a mistake, but I can learn from it and do better next time."

5. Practice self-compassion:

When negative self-talk arises, practice self-compassion by speaking to yourself as you would to a good friend. Offer yourself kind and supportive words, and recognize that mistakes and setbacks are a natural part of the learning and growing process. Treat yourself with the same kindness and understanding that you would offer to someone you care about.

8.2 Examples of Daily Self-love Practices

Self-love practices are essential for our physical, mental, and emotional well-being. By incorporating daily self-love practices into our routine, we can cultivate a more positive and compassionate relationship with ourselves.

Here are some examples of daily self-love practices:

Gratitude journaling is a simple and effective way to cultivate gratitude and positivity in our lives. By taking a few minutes each day to write down things we are grateful for, we can shift our focus towards the positive aspects of our life and cultivate a sense of gratitude.

Mindful breathing is another powerful self-love practice that can help to reduce stress and increase mindfulness. By taking a few deep breaths and focusing on our breathing, we can be fully present in the moment and cultivate a sense of calm and peace.

Positive affirmations are a powerful way to shift our mindset and boost our self-confidence. By repeating positive affirmations to ourselves throughout the day, such as "I am capable," "I am worthy," or "I am enough," we can cultivate a more positive and compassionate relationship with ourselves.

Self-care practices are essential for our physical, emotional, and mental well-being. Engaging in activities that promote self-care, such as exercise, meditation, journaling, or spending time with loved ones, can help to reduce stress and increase our sense of well-being.

Setting boundaries is another important self-love practice that can help to prioritize our needs and desires. By saying no to activities or situations that do not serve our well-being, we can prioritize our own needs and cultivate a sense of self-respect and self-care.

Engaging in hobbies and passions is also important for our self-love practice. By setting aside time each day to pursue hobbies and interests that bring us joy and fulfillment, we can cultivate a sense of purpose and meaning in our lives.

Finally, practicing mindful eating can help to cultivate a more positive and loving relationship with our bodies. By paying attention to the flavors, textures, and sensations of our food, and savoring each bite, we can practice mindful eating and cultivate a sense of gratitude and appreciation for our bodies.

An example of a typical day of self-love practice:

Morning:

Start the day by saying positive affirmations to yourself, such as "I am capable and worthy of achieving my goals."

Take a few minutes to stretch and do some gentle yoga or meditation to help calm your mind and set a positive tone for the day ahead.

Make a healthy breakfast that nourishes your body and fuels your mind.

Afternoon:

Take a break from work and go for a walk outside to get some fresh air and exercise.

Practice mindful breathing exercises to help reduce stress and increase relaxation.

Take time to connect with a friend or loved one and share positive thoughts and feelings.

Evening:

Take a warm bath or shower to help relax your body and mind.

Write down three things you're grateful for from your day.

Treat yourself to a relaxing activity such as reading a book, watching a movie, or doing something creative.

By incorporating these self-love practices into your daily routine, you can develop a more positive and compassionate relationship with yourself, reduce stress and anxiety, and cultivate greater overall well-being.

8.3 The Transformative Power of Self-love in Achieving your Goals

Self-love is a powerful force that can transform our lives in numerous ways, including helping us to achieve our goals. When we have a strong sense of self-love, we are more likely to believe in ourselves and our abilities, which can help us to overcome obstacles and pursue our dreams with greater confidence and determination.

One way that self-love can help us achieve our goals is by increasing our motivation. When we truly love and value ourselves, we are more likely to prioritize our goals and put in the effort required to achieve them. We are also more likely to persist in the face of setbacks and failures, as we understand that these experiences are a natural part of the learning and growing process.

Another way that self-love can help us achieve our goals is by increasing our resilience. When we love ourselves, we are better equipped to handle the challenges and stresses that come with pursuing our goals. We are more likely to bounce back from setbacks and failures, and we are less likely to give up when things get tough.

Self-love can also help us to set healthier and more realistic goals. When we love ourselves, we are more attuned to our own needs and desires, and we are better able to set goals that are aligned with our values and priorities. This can help us to avoid burnout and achieve a greater sense of fulfillment and satisfaction in our lives.

Self-talk to put Positive Self-talk into Practice

I can start small by complimenting myself for a job well done or offering words of encouragement during a challenging moment. Consistency is key, so I will set aside time each day to practice positive self-talk. I can also use visual cues by posting positive affirmations or reminders in visible places to help me stay mindful of my self-talk throughout the day. It's important to monitor my self-talk and challenge negative thoughts by reframing them into positive affirmations or constructive feedback. When negative self-talk arises, I will practice self-compassion by speaking to myself as I would to a good friend and offering kind and supportive words. By consistently practicing these self-love habits, I can transform my mindset and achieve my goals with confidence and self-assurance.

Conclusion

Key Points:

1. Self-love is a journey that requires intentional practice and patience.

2. Positive self-talk is a powerful tool for building self-love and confidence.

3. Self-love involves recognizing and embracing your unique qualities and strengths, and practicing self-compassion and forgiveness.

4. Building a supportive environment and engaging in self-care practices can also help to cultivate self-love.

Final Thoughts

Self-love is not a one-time achievement, but a continuous journey of growth and self-discovery. It requires intentional effort and patience, as well as a willingness to challenge negative self-talk and embrace one's unique qualities and strengths.

By practicing positive self-talk, engaging in self-care practices, and surrounding oneself with supportive influences, it is possible to cultivate a strong sense of self-love and confidence.

Remember that self-love is a journey, not a destination, and that it is never too late to begin practicing self-love and embracing your unique qualities and strengths.

Encouragement

I encourage you to continue on the journey of self-love and self-discovery. Celebrate your strengths, challenge negative self-talk, and practice self-compassion and forgiveness. Remember that you are worthy of love and acceptance, and that you have the power to create a supportive and positive environment for yourself.

Bibliography

- Neff, K. (2011). Self-compassion: Stop Beating Yourself Up and Leave Insecurity Behind. New York, NY: William Morrow Paperbacks.

- Germer, C. K. (2009). The Mindful Path to Self-Compassion: Freeing Yourself from Destructive Thoughts and Emotions. New York, NY: The Guilford Press.

- Rosenberg, M. (2015). Nonviolent Communication: A Language of Life. Encinitas, CA: Puddledancer Press.

- Kristin, N., & Harris, A. H. (2013). The Science of Self-Compassion. In J. Seppälä, E. Simon-Thomas, S. Brown, M. C. Worline, C. D. Cameron, & J. R. Doty (Eds.), The Oxford Handbook of Compassion Science (pp. 37-46). New York, NY: Oxford University Press.

- Gilbert, P. (2010). The Compassionate Mind: A New Approach to Life's Challenges. Oakland, CA: New Harbinger Publications.

- Burns, D. D. (1999). The Feeling Good Handbook. Penguin Random House.

- Emmons, R. A. (2007). Thanks!: How the New Science of Gratitude Can Make You Happier. Houghton Mifflin Harcourt.

- Hayes, S. C., Strosahl, K. D., & Wilson, K. G. (2011). Acceptance and Commitment Therapy: The Process and Practice of Mindful Change. Guilford Press.

- Jay, M. (2018). This is Your Brain on Joy: A Revolutionary Program for Balancing Mood, Restoring Brain Health, and

Nurturing Spiritual Growth. Faith Words.

- Schiraldi, G. R. (2017). The Self-Esteem Workbook. New Harbinger Publications.

- Rosenberg, M. (2015). The Gifts of Imperfection: Let Go of Who You Think You're Supposed to Be and Embrace Who You Are. Center City, MN: Hazelden Publishing.

- Gilbert, P. (2010). The Compassionate Mind: A New Approach to Life's Challenges. Oakland, CA: New Harbinger Publications.

- Brown, B. (2007). I Thought It Was Just Me (but it isn't): Telling the Truth About Perfectionism, Inadequacy, and Power. New York: Penguin Random House.

- Fredrickson, B. L. (2009). Positivity: Top-Notch Research Reveals the Upward Spiral That Will Change Your Life. Three Rivers Press.

- Seligman, M. E. P. (2011). Flourish: A Visionary New Understanding of Happiness and Well-being. Free Press.

- Rosenberg, M. (2015). The Power of Self-Love: Building a Relationship with Yourself That Changes Everything. New World Library.

- Dweck, C. S. (2007). Mindset: The New Psychology of Success. Ballantine Books.

- Kristin Neff, Self-Compassion: The Proven Power of Being Kind to Yourself, 2011

- Louise Hay, You Can Heal Your Life, 1984

- Carol S. Dweck, Mindset: The New Psychology of Success, 2006

- Brene Brown, The Gifts of Imperfection: Let Go of Who You Think You're Supposed to Be and Embrace Who You Are,

2010

- Martin E.P. Seligman, Learned Optimism: How to Change Your Mind and Your Life, 1990

- Shad Helmstetter, What to Say When You Talk to Your Self, 1986

- McGonigal, K. (2019). The joy of movement: How exercise helps us find happiness, hope, connection, and courage. Penguin.

www.ingramcontent.com/pod-product-compliance
Lightning Source LLC
Chambersburg PA
CBHW060516280326
41933CB00014B/2991